Doers and Dreamers
social reformers
of the nineteenth century

Lynne Deur

Lerner Publications Company • Minneapolis, Minnesota

Doers and Dreamers
social reformers
of the **nineteenth century**

Lynne Deur

ACKNOWLEDGMENTS: The illustrations are reproduced through the courtesy of: pp. 3, 71, 73, Maine Historical Society; p. 4, NBC photo; pp. 6, 8, Indiana Historical Society Library; p. 11, Indiana Department of Natural Resources; pp. 13, 33, 46, 51, *Dictionary of American Portraits*, Dover Publications, Inc.; pp. 14, 17, Fruitlands Museums; pp. 19, 23, 24, Perkins School For The Blind; pp. 26, 28, 29, 32, Oneida Ltd. Silversmiths; p. 35, The New York Academy of Medicine; pp. 37, 80, 82, 83, 84, Independent Picture Service; pp. 38, 43, 60, 64, 69, 77, Library of Congress; p. 40, National Park Service, United States Department of the Interior; p. 45, Sophia Smith Collection, Smith College Library; pp. 49, 57, 63, 67, 76, 79, Arthur and Elizabeth Schlesinger Library on the History of Women in America; p. 87, Wallace Kirkland.

Front Cover: Courtesy Chicago Historical Society.

Back Cover: Library of Congress.

LIBRARY OF CONGRESS CATALOGING IN PUBLICATION DATA

Deur, Lynne.
Doers and dreamers.

(A Pull Ahead Book)
SUMMARY: Brief biographies of fourteen nineteenth-century men and women involved in such reform movements as women's rights, temperance, and the abolition of slavery.

1. U. S.—Social conditions. 2. U. S.—Biography—Juvenile literature. [1. U. S.—Social conditions. 2. U. S.—Biography] I. Title.

HV27.D47   361'.92'2 [B] [920]   79-128808
ISBN 0-8225-0462-6

International Standard Book Number: 0-8225-0462-6
Library of Congress Catalog Card Number: 79-128808

contents

Neal Dow

The March on Washington for Jobs and Freedom, August 1963

Introduction

Today is a time of social unrest. Protest marches, reform movements, and riots make newspaper headlines almost daily. But social change is not new to our country, or to our time. A quick look at American history reveals that social reform in the United States began long before the 20th century. The 19th century, for example, witnessed an especially colorful parade of protestors and social reformers. This book is about a handful of the most interesting and important of these people. Many were dedicated and courageous. Others were simply misguided dreamers.

The reformers of the 19th century fought for a great many social reforms, including women's rights, temperance, and the abolition of slavery. Some, like Robert Owen and John Noyes, tried to create perfect societies, free from evil. Others, like Dorothea Dix and Samuel Howe, spent their energies trying to make life more bearable for the sick and handicapped. While their goals differed, the reformers all had one thing in common: they were radicals in their own time. They clamored for, worked for, and even suffered for reforms that today we take for granted. Often stubborn and laughable, they nevertheless dared to live their impossible dreams.

Robert Owen

Robert Owen
(1771-1858)

In 1824 a ship from Great Britain arrived in New York City carrying the wealthy industrialist and social reformer Robert Owen. Owen was already well known for his reform work in Great Britain. There he had created a model town and had helped fight abuses suffered by factory workers, many of whom were children. But Owen was not satisfied. He dreamed of creating a perfect community, a new society free from the evils he saw in the existing social system. America, Owen felt, was the ideal place to experiment with a model community. Certainly this young country would be willing to accept new ideas.

Owen selected a town named Harmonie in southwestern Indiana for his experiment. Harmonie had been established in 1814 by George Rapp and his followers, a group of religious dissenters from the Lutheran Church. Eager to begin his experiment, Robert Owen bought the community and renamed it New Harmony.

A drawing of New Harmony, Robert Owen's model community

Robert Owen based his plans for New Harmony on a belief more accepted today than in the early 1800s. Owen was convinced that a man should not be blamed if he was ignorant and wicked, or praised if he was intelligent and good. He believed that the circumstances surrounding a man's life should be praised or blamed, not the man. Improve the circumstances and surroundings that mold a man's life, he concluded, and you will improve the man.

Owen also believed that struggle and competition between men had to be replaced with cooperation and equal opportunity for all. To put his ideas into action, Owen prepared a constitution for New Harmony. It said that each man at New Harmony was to be independent but was to promote "the happiness of the world." It also provided that each man would own an equal share of the community, sharing both the work and the profits. Equality was actually limited, however, since the constitution clearly stated that "persons of color" were expected to look for happiness elsewhere.

People of many different types flocked to New Harmony. Some came because New Harmony offered freedom of religion. Others came because they saw in New Harmony the opportunity to live the easy life. The odd mixture of people who fled to New Harmony was, in part, the cause of its failure. Jealousy and distrust grew rapidly among the various religious groups, and too few people were willing to put in an honest day's work.

Owen was hopeful, despite these early difficulties. To help insure New Harmony's success, he persuaded an impressive group of teachers and scientists from Europe and the United States to join him in his community. Among those who came was his son, Robert Dale Owen, who later became an editor of the New Harmony *Gazette*. With the help of these professionals, Robert Owen and New Harmony achieved some major successes. New Harmony's leaders established the first kindergarten and the first free public school system in America. They also established the first trade school, the first free public library, and the first woman's club.

Members of New Harmony delighted in simple amusements, like trying to find their way in and out of this winding maze of hedges.

Even with these successes, New Harmony was headed for failure. The community lacked the organization and purpose Owen had hoped for. Only a few of New Harmony's members understood his aims. Owen was absent from New Harmony more than he was present, and without his personal leadership, even his most faithful followers lost enthusiasm. Another serious problem was that New Harmony didn't have enough farmers and craftsmen to provide the people with the food and clothing they needed.

These were not the only problems faced by New Harmony. Owen's opposition to the private ownership of property and the institutions of marriage and religion also contributed to the community's collapse. His open remarks about these "monstrous evils," as he called them, drew much criticism. As a result, New Harmony became known as a place for atheism and free love.

By 1827 New Harmony's failure was complete, and Robert Owen's plan for America was doomed. Owen himself suffered great financial loss. He returned to England, willing to admit that a perfect community required a select group of people, trained for such an experiment.

Until his death in 1858, Owen remained a devoted reformer. The few years he spent at New Harmony were only a small part of his long, active life, but his noble experiment there earned him the name "father of American socialism."

Robert Owen cared about mankind. He failed to create a new and better world at New Harmony, but he lived to convince others that the need for a kinder society did exist.

Amos Bronson Alcott

Amos Bronson Alcott
(1799-1888)

A reformer is usually thought of as an idealist—a person who dreams of making the world perfect. Many people of the 19th century thought of reformers as fanatics who simply could not face the realities of life. Generally, such opinions were unfair, but not always. Amos Bronson Alcott, New England reformer and philosopher, truly was a fanatical idealist. Alcott had no time for the hard realities of life. He was too busy dreaming and discussing his impossible dreams.

In his classroom at Temple School, Bronson Alcott experimented with many new methods of teaching.

Bronson Alcott, as he was usually called, was born in Connecticut in 1799. His family was poor, and by the age of 14, young Alcott was working in a clock factory. Later he became a peddler of almanacs and trinkets.

Amos Bronson Alcott was a self-educated man, and he had ideas on many subjects. He thrived on discussion and conversation. So no one was surprised when he turned to teaching. It was as a teacher that Bronson Alcott made his most important contributions to the world of reform.

Alcott would have been at home in the modern classroom. In his Temple School in Boston, established in 1834, he put into practice some of his theories about learning. Education, he believed, was more than the process of filling students with facts. Alcott was convinced that the whole child should be involved in the learning process.

To prove his educational theories, Alcott began by treating his young students as people. He replaced their backbreaking benches with chairs and desks. He shocked the public by giving his students gymnastic exercises. He brought paintings into the classroom and introduced his pupils to the excitement of good fiction. He invited a Negro girl into the school. Most important, he encouraged students to think for themselves. Because of his experiments, Bronson Alcott was not very popular in old Boston. But his ideas about learning had a lasting and important influence on later developments in American education.

Except in his teaching career, Alcott was not an active reformer. In fact, he taught that most attempts to reform society were quite useless. He believed that change, reform, had to begin within each person. People were basically good, he believed. When men reformed within and behaved as Nature intended, evil would disappear.

Bronson Alcott decided to experiment in living as Nature intended. He would start a small community where he and a few others could live an ideal life. Experimenting in communal living was popular at the time, and Alcott had to try it for himself. Thus, in 1844 he established the ideal community of Fruitlands near Harvard, Massachusetts. The Fruitlands family was made up of about 12 adults, one of them Mrs. Alcott. Also included were the four Alcott girls.

Fruitlands was destined to be a disaster. Bronson Alcott personally set the rules for the community, and he demanded that all Fruitlanders be strict vegetarians. Even eggs, butter, cheese, and milk were forbidden. There was to be no use of products like tea, cotton, and coffee, which were produced by slave labor. All food, in fact, had to be raised at Fruitlands.

Alcott's strict rules made farming at Fruitlands very difficult. Oxen or horses could not be used to plow the fields.

Bronson Alcott and the other members of his small community at Fruitlands lived together as one family in this house.

Weeds could not be pulled in the vegetable garden. After all, Alcott reasoned, hadn't the weeds as much right to grow as the vegetables? The selection of vegetables to be planted was also important. Alcott wanted to raise only plants that grew upward toward the sun. He considered roots and bulbs that buried themselves in the earth to be unfit food for human beings.

Once the crops were planted, late in the season, Mrs. Alcott and the girls were put in charge of the farming.

The men were occupied with more important matters — discussing ideas, dreaming about the future. When the few crops that did manage to grow were ready to be harvested, Bronson Alcott and the other men went off to a lecture in Boston. From there they visited other communities. In their absence, Mrs. Alcott and three of the girls, the oldest 13, saved what crops they could by working in cold, driving wind and rain.

Fruitlands failed miserably. After a mere seven months in their ideal community, Alcott and his family were left with no food. Then friends came to the rescue. But in spite of this bitter failure, Bronson Alcott was not "reformed" into living a more normal life. Since it apparently did not occur to him that he should support his family, their needs were provided for by a close friend, the philosopher Ralph Waldo Emerson.

In later years, Alcott's daughter Louisa May (the author of *Little Women*) supported the family. Louisa had often lost patience with her father. She had watched her mother struggle to keep the family together and finally die from overwork. Nevertheless, Miss Alcott took such good care of her father that he referred to her as "Duty's Child."

Bronson Alcott died in 1888, just a few months after the death of his famous daughter. Alcott was indeed an idealist. Some of his ideas were laughable. The best ones, such as his educational reforms, were ahead of his time.

Samuel Gridley Howe

Samuel Gridley Howe
(1801-1876)

"My father had always something of the soldier about him—a quick, active step, gallant bearing, and a voice tender, yet strong. . . ." This was the way Florence Howe Hall remembered her father, Samuel Gridley Howe. Howe was a born reformer—dashing, intelligent, a natural leader. He was a man who followed his conscience, even if it meant breaking the law.

As a young man Howe graduated from Harvard Medical School. But settling down into medical practice did not interest him. Instead he traveled to Greece in 1824 to aid in that country's War of Independence against Turkey. He spent six years in Greece, serving as both a soldier and a surgeon. When Howe returned to the United States, he raised money for the Greek cause and sent food and clothing to the war-torn country.

Howe then became involved with Dr. John Fisher, a well-known Boston physician. Dr. Fisher was looking for a man to help him establish a school for the blind. He needed someone daring and enthusiastic, someone to help those who had been neglected for so long. Young Dr. Howe was just the man Fisher was looking for. Excited by Fisher's ideas, Howe traveled to Europe again—this time to visit a number of outstanding European schools for the blind. In 1832 Howe returned to Boston with two experienced teachers.

With the aid of the teachers, Samuel Howe organized the New England Asylum for the Blind. First set up in Howe's own home, the school originally had only six pupils. They ranged from six to twenty years of age. Howe took his new challenge seriously. Much of the time he wore a blindfold so that he could better understand the problems of his pupils. Howe spent many of his nights gluing twine to cardboard, forming letters, numbers, and maps that the blind students could "read" with their hands. His line-type was used widely by the blind until the Braille system was later invented.

When money for his school ran out, Howe was faced with one of the most challenging tasks of his career—gaining public support for the blind. Most people believed that the blind were hopelessly handicapped and that trying to help them was a useless task. Dr. Howe decided to show the public how much the blind could learn. In front of the Massachusetts State Legislature, two of his students read aloud by moving their fingers over the raised letters Howe had developed. The blind, Howe demonstrated, could be helped after all.

Howe and his students gave similar demonstrations elsewhere. Soon a group of impressed women held a fair and raised a large sum of money for the school. Then Thomas Handasyd Perkins, a wealthy merchant, donated a mansion. Howe's school, which he renamed the Perkins Institution for the Blind, was firmly established.

Perkins Institution was not the last of Samuel Howe's accomplishments. The nation was greatly impressed when Howe succeeded in teaching Laura Bridgman to read and write. Laura was not only blind, but deaf and mute as well. The fact that she had been taught to read and write was the first glimmer of hope for others who lived in a dark and silent world.

Although Samuel Howe served as the head of Perkins Institution for 44 years, other crusades and reform movements drew his attention as well. He served as the chairman of the Massachusetts state board of charities from 1865 to 1874. During this time he strongly supported Dorothea Dix in her crusade for better care for the insane. An abolitionist, Howe was also involved in the crusade against slavery. In 1848 he helped organize the Free-Soil Party.

This mansion, which became Perkins Institution for the Blind, was donated to Samuel Howe by Thomas Handasyd Perkins in 1833.

This political party opposed the admission of any new slave states into the Union.

Toward the end of his life, Samuel Howe's fame dwindled. When the name "Howe" was mentioned, most people immediately thought of his wife Julia. She became a heroine to Americans by writing "The Battle Hymn of the Republic," and her fame grew steadily. Historians suspect that the marriage of the two famous Howes was not the happiest.

Still in existence, the Perkins Institution for the Blind
has helped thousands of handicapped people.

Samuel asked his wife for a divorce to marry a younger
woman, but he never got it. Evidently Mrs. Howe was not
willing to give her husband up. This is the way she described
him in a poem:

> A great grieved heart, an iron will,
>   As fearless blood as ever ran.
> A form elate with nervous strength
>   And fibrous vigor,—all man.

Samuel Gridley Howe died in 1876. He never achieved
the national recognition won by his wife, but he would
long be remembered for his dedicated work in helping
the blind.

•

John Humphrey Noyes
(1811-1886)

In 1830 a tall, thin boy graduated from Dartmouth College with highest honors. John Humphrey Noyes had originally planned to practice law. However, attending a religious revival meeting in 1831 changed both his plans and his life. During the meeting Noyes heard the great evangelist Charles Grandison Finney claim that human perfection was possible on earth. Man, Finney said, could be saved from sin and live as God meant him to.

Inspired by Finney's religious beliefs, Noyes decided to quit law and take up theology. After studying at Andover and Yale Theological seminaries, John Humphrey Noyes became a minister. Noyes, however, was not a typical 19th-century clergyman. His unusual ideas about religion and society eventually led to the founding of the Oneida Community. This was one of the most successful communistic settlements in American history.

John Humphrey Noyes

The religious beliefs of John Humphrey Noyes were shockingly different from those of most Protestant ministers. Instead of looking forward to Christ's Second Coming, he believed it had already occurred in 70 A.D. According to Noyes, this event made it possible for man to achieve perfection on earth. Noyes announced that he himself had reached the supreme state of human perfection in 1834. He believed that he was free from sin, and also free to break the laws of an imperfect society.

Noyes's unusual views on various subjects soon got him into trouble. He lost a teaching position, and his license to preach was suspended. But Noyes did not give up his beliefs. In 1836 he founded a community in Putney, Vermont, based on his theory of "perfectionism." The Putney experiment lasted almost 10 years. It ended in a dispute over the unusual marriage system practiced by the community's inhabitants. Noyes was accused of adultery, a serious crime in those days. He had to get out of town, and the Putney Community broke up.

Noyes was not discouraged by the failure of his first experiment in communal living. In 1848 he established another community, near Oneida, New York. Noyes and his 87 followers called themselves Perfectionists. They were also known as "Bible communists" because they rejected the private ownership of property. In their opinion, private property encouraged selfishness and rivalry. To avoid these evils, the Perfectionists shared all their possessions and lived together as one family.

Members of the Oneida Community in front of their living quarters, 1860

The Oneida Community grew rapidly. At first the Perfectionists made their living by farming and lumbering. But Noyes knew that other communities like Oneida had failed because of their dedication to the ideal farm life. He knew that if Oneida were to survive, it would need industry. Carefully Noyes developed a plan. He convinced an old trapper in the community to share his secret of making fine steel traps. The Oneida steel trap soon became well known throughout the country. It brought the Oneida Community financial security. In one year alone, profits from the sale of the traps amounted to $80,000.

The Oneida steel trap became well known throughout the
country and brought the community financial security.

The steel trap business was only one of the successful
industries at Oneida. Noyes and his followers also estab-
blished a canning factory. They manufactured silk thread,
as well as the machinery used to make it. Finally, they
began to produce the famous Oneida silverware.

John Humphrey Noyes had a real genius for organization and leadership. In addition to developing successful
businesses, he kept his society of Perfectionists running
amazingly well. A labor committee established by Noyes
matched the members up to the jobs for which they were
best suited. The committee made sure that no one stayed on
an undesirable job for more than two months. When there
was more work than the Perfectionists could handle, Noyes
hired outsiders to help.

Noyes realized that many communal societies had crumbled because of fights and squabbles among community members. In order to prevent this from happening at Oneida, Noyes set up a system of "mutual criticism." The Perfectionists were encouraged to criticize each other and settle their differences openly at meetings held before the entire community. This practice prevented small quarrels from growing into community feuds.

Perhaps the most radical of Noyes's ideas put into practice at Oneida was that of complex marriage. Noyes rejected conventional marriage because he believed the small family unit encouraged selfishness. In complex marriage, everyone in the community was considered married to everyone else. Sexual activity, however, was strictly supervised by a special committee. Birth control was practiced, and when a couple wished to have a baby, they had to get the permission of the committee. Permission was given only after serious consideration. John Noyes believed that only people with good minds and good bodies should have children. He believed that this was the way to raise the healthiest, most intelligent children. After the children were born, they were raised by a special children's center, not by their parents.

The practice of complex marriage at Oneida drew much criticism and eventually led to the community's downfall. When Noyes was threatened with arrest because of the marriage system at Oneida, he fled to Canada. From there he urged the Perfectionists to give up complex marriage for the good of the community. He did not, however, reject the idea. The world simply was not ready for complex marriage, Noyes reasoned.

This silverware is a product of Oneida Silversmiths, the company founded by John Noyes and his followers.

In 1881, approximately 30 years after Oneida was founded, the Perfectionists broke up as a community. But many of them became stockholders and employees in Oneida Silversmiths, a thriving company which is still in existence. John Noyes remained in Canada until his death in 1886. His experiment at Oneida was labeled everything from a "brilliant success" to a "utopia of obscenity." But public opinion mattered little to Noyes. He lived and died true to his beliefs.

Dorothea Dix

Dorothea Dix

(1802-1887)

On a cold day in March of 1841, a tall, handsome woman named Dorothea Dix was asked to teach Sunday School in a Massachusetts jail. While at the jail she discovered that insane persons were also kept there—locked in a cold, damp cellar. Her visit with these unfortunate people was a great turning point in Dorothea's life. She pledged to help those she had seen and others like them. It was a pledge that made her one of America's greatest reformers.

Dorothea Dix was 40 years old when she visited that Massachusetts jail. Before then her life had been rather uneventful. Her father was a wandering preacher who enjoyed drinking as much as preaching. He visited the taverns in every village and town he traveled through. Young Dorothea traveled with her parents and handed out religious pamphlets during her father's sermons.

By the age of 12, Dorothea could no longer stand the laughter and jeers her father's sermons so often received. So she ran away to live with her grandmother in Boston. The elderly woman gave Dorothea a good education and insisted that she learn to be a proper lady. Her grandmother provided for all of Dorothea's material needs, but gave the girl little real love or affection. For Dorothea, it was a lonely life.

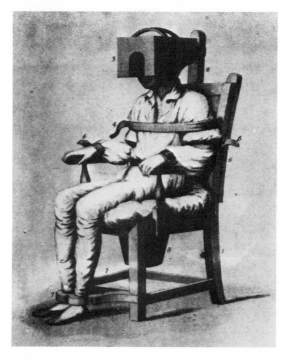

Instruments of torture like this "tranquillizing chair" were used to treat the mentally ill in the 1800s.

Until Miss Dix visited the Massachusetts jail in 1841, she had been a schoolteacher and had traveled at length in Europe. Dorothea had no real need to work, since she had inherited a great deal of money from her grandmother. However, her visit to the jail made her realize how badly the insane needed help. There were only a few scattered hospitals for the insane and mentally ill. Most of these people were kept in jails or boarded out to anyone who would take care of them. Aware of their suffering, Dorothea decided that she would help the insane.

Miss Dix began her crusade for the insane by visiting jails throughout the state of Massachusetts. In every jail she visited, the mentally ill were kept and cared for worse than animals. Even the mildly disturbed were treated like hardened criminals. In a detailed notebook of her visits, Miss Dix told of a man chained in a tiny, dark, frost-covered room. She told of others who were chained and beaten with rods.

In 1843 Dorothea Dix presented a report of her findings to the Massachusetts State Legislature. In it she wrote:

> I proceed, gentlemen, briefly to call your attention to the present state of insane persons confined within this Commonwealth; in cages, closets, cellars, stalls, pens; chained, naked, beaten with rods, and lashed into obedience.

The report caused an uproar. There were many who wished to quiet Miss Dix. But she had important supporters, such as Samuel Gridley Howe. Hundreds read her report in the newspapers. The state legislature was forced to act. Very soon 200 rooms were added to the small state hospital for the mentally ill that existed in Massachusetts.

One of Dorothea Dix's greatest accomplishments was the founding of the New Jersey State Hospital, which she called her "first born child."

After her success in Massachusetts, Dorothea Dix went on to establish New Jersey's first hospital for the insane. She then continued her crusade throughout the United States. Her visits were not pleasant and often demanded great courage. In one dungeon the keeper begged her not to approach a man in chains, claiming that the man would "tear her limb from limb." Dorothea ignored the warning. She went to the man gently, calling him by name. Instead of flying into a rage, the man wept. Dorothea ordered him washed and put in a clean room. Two months later that "dangerous lunatic" was doing helpful tasks around a state hospital.

As the Superintendent of Nurses for the Union army, Dorothea Dix worked in many field hospitals like this one during the Civil War.

Dorothea Dix taught the entire world a lesson. The mentally ill were not dangerous beasts. They were human beings who needed care like other sick people. They needed doctors and nurses and hospitals. Amazingly enough, Dorothea Dix taught the world this lesson without ever becoming well known herself. She made friends with people of importance and wealth to obtain whatever support she needed. Dorothea Dix did not want fame; she wanted reform.

During the Civil War Dorothea took some time out in her work for the insane. She served as the Superintendent of Nurses for the Union army. Many who worked with Miss Dix complained, for she was very strict and demanding. One of the nurses under her command was Louisa May Alcott. She described Dorothea Dix as a "kind soul, but queer and arbitrary."

After the war, Dorothea continued to make demands on herself and on others. She visited the hospitals she had helped establish. Many times her visits were unannounced so that she could accurately judge the conditions in each hospital. Until the age of 80, she continued to travel throughout the world to encourage reform in the treatment of the insane. She also led the crusade to improve prison conditions and the treatment of criminals.

Finally, at the age of 80, Miss Dix retired. For five years she lived in a room set aside for her at the New Jersey hospital she had established. Then, in 1887, Dorothea Dix died. She had spent her life in the service of those who could not help themselves, and she had asked nothing for herself. Dorothea Dix would go down in history as one of the greatest reformers of the 19th century.

Frederick Douglass

Frederick Douglass
(1817-1895)

It was January of 1842. A tall, broad-shouldered black man stood before a meeting of the Massachusetts Anti-Slavery Society. "I appear before the immense assembly this evening," he began, "as a thief and a robber. I stole this head, these limbs, this body from my master, and ran off with them." The man was Frederick Douglass, a runaway slave who became a great reformer and one of the most respected men of his time.

Frederick Douglass was born the son of Harriet Bailey, a slave, and an unknown white father. Douglass felt the sorrows of slavery early in life. He was separated from his mother shortly after birth. He spent the first few years of life with his grandmother, but was separated from her too when he was sent to another farm. One of the happiest moments in young Frederick's life came when he was re-united with his mother. The meeting between the mother and son was brief, and it was to be their last. Frederick later recalled it:

> My mother had walked twelve miles to see me, and had the same distance to travel again before morning sunrise. I do not remember seeing her again. Her death soon ended the little communication that had existed between us, and with it, I believe, a life full of weariness and heartfelt sorrow.

Being forced to live apart from those he loved created in Douglass a deep and silent hatred of slavery. Yet, Frederick Douglass was more fortunate than most slaves. At a young age he was sold to a family named Auld in Baltimore. His job was to watch over the Auld's young son. Mrs. Auld was fond of Frederick. Innocently, she began to teach him the alphabet. He learned quickly. However, when Mrs. Auld boasted of the young slave's achievements to her husband, the lessons were stopped. Mr. Auld was furious. Slaves were to be kept ignorant so that they would not desire freedom. But Frederick was intelligent and had learned "too much" already. Patiently he taught himself to read and write.

As a young man, Douglass was owned by many masters. Other slaves respected him for his intelligence and ability to read and write. But slavemasters distrusted and feared him. One day, when Douglass could no longer endure the beatings from a harsh master, a fight broke out between the two men. After a long struggle, Douglass defeated his opponent. Never again did the slavemaster lay a hand on him. It was a turning point in Douglass' life: "I was a changed being after that fight. I was nothing before; I was a man now. . . . I had reached the point at which I was not afraid to die. This spirit made me a free man in fact, though I still remained a slave in form."

This songsheet cover celebrates Frederick Douglass's escape from slavery. "The Fugitive's Song" was dedicated to Douglass, and described him as a graduate of the "peculiar institution" of slavery.

In 1838, several years after the eventful fight, Douglass finally managed to escape from slavery to the free state of Massachusetts. Three years later, after he had married and settled down, Douglass appeared before a meeting of the Massachusetts Anti-Slavery Society. For the first time in his life, he publicly spoke about his life as a former slave. Douglass so impressed the audience that he was hired as a regular speaker.

Frederick Douglass soon became one of the most famous orators in America. He traveled throughout the Northeast, telling of his life as a slave. Instead of simply describing his own experiences, Douglass began to attack the institution of slavery in general. The impact of his speeches was great. Soon listeners began to doubt that the tall, intelligent Negro had ever been a slave at all. To settle their growing doubts, Douglass wrote his memoirs, *Narrative of the Life of Frederick Douglass*. Published in 1845, the book became a best seller in America and Europe.

After the publication of his book, Douglass lectured for nearly two years in the British Isles. His appearances there earned him a large following and enough money to buy his freedom from his former master. (As a runaway slave, he could have been captured and returned to slavery at any time.) In 1847 Frederick Douglass returned to America a free man. He then established the *North Star*, a weekly newspaper which urged the abolition of slavery.

In addition to editing his paper and lecturing, Douglass worked in other ways to end slavery and bring about equal rights for blacks. He served as president of the New England Anti-Slavery Society and helped other slaves escape to freedom by taking part in the Underground Railroad. When the Civil War broke out, Douglass organized two regiments of Massachusetts Negroes to serve in the Union army. Among those he recruited were his own sons.

In his later years, Frederick Douglass filled various government posts, including those of minister to Haiti and marshall of the District of Columbia.

Frederick Douglass won the respect of thousands as an orator, as a reformer, as a man. In his autobiography, *The Life and Times of Frederick Douglass*, he wrote: "While I cannot boast of having accomplished great things in the world, I cannot on the other hand feel that I have lived in vain." In 1895 the man who had risen from the sorrows and brutalities of slavery to great public esteem passed away. Certainly, he had not lived in vain.

Lucy Stone

Lucy Stone
(1818-1893)

Mr. Stone was a wealthy Massachusetts farmer. He managed his farm and family with an iron fist. Mrs. Stone worked long and hard. On one particular evening in 1818, she milked the cows and then fed the hungry crew who were helping the Stones hay. That same night she gave birth to a daughter, Lucy.

Lucy Stone was a born rebel. At a very young age she was angered by what life had to offer her. Because she was a girl, she would not receive much education. At an early age she would become a wife, subject to her husband's authority. She would work hard, have baby after baby, and die young. She was a 19th-century woman—a woman with no rights. But Lucy Stone was no ordinary girl. She was determined to make life better, both for herself and for other women.

After teaching school for a time, Lucy decided to go to college. She chose Oberlin, a famous college in Ohio. Her father, who preferred that his daughter get married, did not approve. But Lucy was not to be stopped by her father's opinions. She attended Oberlin, working to pay her way for the first two years. Finally, Mr. Stone gave in. His daughter was a good student and a natural leader. He agreed to pay her way for the two years remaining until graduation. In 1847 Lucy Stone became the first woman from New England to graduate from college.

But Lucy wanted more than a college education. She was burning with desire to help secure freedom for both women and slaves. In 1847 Lucy Stone made history by becoming the first American woman to lecture on women's rights. Her crusade for abolition began a year later when she was hired as a lecturer for the Massachusetts Anti-Slavery Society. Lucy was perfect for the job. She knew how to use her low, vibrant voice most dramatically, and she was firm in her beliefs. Many times she was mobbed and laughed at by her audiences, but she did not give up. There were few cities or villages in the East and Midwest that were not visited by Lucy Stone.

Lucy did not marry until 1855, when she was 37. Her husband, Henry Brown Blackwell, was also a reformer. The wedding was not an ordinary one. Lucy and Henry rewrote the marriage vows. Present marriage laws, the couple felt, were out of date. The wife could own no property, and the husband was granted superior authority in all respects. Upon his death, a husband could will all of his property and even the children away from his wife. Lucy Stone and Henry Blackwell wrote a marriage contract that declared them equals. The first married woman to keep her maiden name, Mrs. Lucy Stone promised to love her husband but did not vow to obey him. In one way, however, the wedding was a very ordinary one—the bride cried.

One of the first important feminist magazines, *The Woman's Journal* was founded by Lucy Stone in 1870.

Lucy Stone's life was a full one. When freedom was won for the slaves following the Civil War, Lucy devoted herself to the cause of women's rights. In 1869 she formed the American Woman's Suffrage Association (AWSA), one of the first important feminist organizations in the United States. As the president of AWSA, Mrs. Stone worked through the state legislatures to win the vote for women. A year after establishing AWSA she founded *The Woman's Journal*. This powerful women's rights magazine survived for nearly 50 years.

As a result of her energetic campaign for women's rights, Lucy Stone was laughed at and criticized all her life. But Lucy Stone was determined not to be defeated. She was so determined, in fact, that "Lucy-Stoner" became a word used to describe a woman who knew her own mind.

Lucy died long before women achieved the right to vote. She did, however, see women gain new respect and support. No longer was a woman considered a "freak" when she stepped out of her household and onto a speaker's platform. "Inferior" women were showing that they were not so inferior after all, as they began to enter colleges and professions. Thanks to Lucy Stone, girls faced a brighter future than they once had.

Lucy Stone died in 1893. Born a rebel, she died a rebel as well. Progress was forever Lucy's motto, and after her death she became the first woman in New England to be cremated. Over 1,000 persons attended her funeral. Lucy had made her mark. Just before her death she whispered to her daughter Alice, "Make the world better." These words seem to have guided her own life.

Elizabeth Cady Stanton

Elizabeth Cady Stanton

(1815-1902)

Elizabeth Cady Stanton spent her youth trying to be as much like a boy as possible. She learned to ride and jump her horse expertly. She studied Latin, Greek, and math—subjects then considered suitable for boys only. Elizabeth wanted to be a boy because boys had many privileges girls were denied—education, careers, fame.

Born in 1815, Elizabeth grew up in a large family in Johnstown, New York. Her father was a lawyer and a congressman. After attending Johnstown Academy and the Troy Female Seminary, Elizabeth decided to marry. Her father objected to her choice of husbands—Henry B. Stanton, a journalist and an antislavery leader. But Elizabeth was not to be dominated by either man. She married Henry Stanton in 1840 in spite of her father's opposition, but not until Henry had agreed to omit the word "obey" from the marriage vows.

The Stantons spent their honeymoon in London, where they were to be delegates to the World Anti-Slavery Convention. Elizabeth was shocked when she and the other women delegates were forbidden to enter the main hall of the convention. After all their work for the antislavery cause, the women were allowed only to watch the convention from a distant gallery. Elizabeth discussed the insult with another woman reformer and delegate, Lucretia Mott. Angered by their unfair treatment, they agreed upon the need to call women to action for greater equality.

In 1840 Elizabeth Stanton and other women delegates attended the World Anti-Slavery Convention in London. The women were shocked when they were forced to sit in a gallery separate from the male delegates.

Following the convention the Stantons moved to Boston, where they made their first home and began their family. When the family moved to Seneca Falls, New York, in 1846, Elizabeth Cady Stanton became more aware of a housewife's hardships than ever before. As the mother of lively children, her days were filled with such tiresome tasks as washing and sewing, cooking and baking, and caring for each new baby. As time passed, Elizabeth grew more and more disgusted with her position as a wife, mother, housekeeper, and physician.

Elizabeth Cady Stanton addresses the first Woman's Rights Convention in Seneca Falls, New York, July 19, 1848.

After meeting with Lucretia Mott again in 1848, Mrs. Stanton decided that the time to call women to action had come. With the help of Mrs. Mott, Elizabeth Stanton organized the first Woman's Rights Convention in Seneca Falls, New York. There she helped write a bill of rights for women. In it, she demanded equal rights with men—in colleges, trades, professions, marriage, and courts—as well as in the right to vote. Elizabeth also called for the passage of more liberal divorce laws. When newspapers made fun of the convention and the ideas proposed, Mrs. Stanton began writing replies and lecturing to interested groups. It was the beginning of her long career as a women's rights reformer.

For years Elizabeth Cady Stanton worked with Lucy Stone, Susan B. Anthony, and others for what seemed an impossible dream—the equality of women. Mrs. Stanton was a lively leader with outspoken ideas. A mother of seven children, she felt that housework was largely a waste of time and energy. In one article for a women's magazine she attacked sewing: "It is a continued drain on sight and strength, on health and life, and it should be the study of every woman to do as little of it as possible."

As leaders of the feminist movement, Elizabeth and her close friend and co-worker Susan B. Anthony were radical and militant in their views. Other women were more patient, giving the nation time to accept the idea of a woman as something more than a slave to babies and household activities. Serious disagreement broke out among the women's rights reformers in 1869. Elizabeth Stanton and Susan Anthony were impatient with the slow-moving methods of Lucy Stone, president of the American Woman's Suffrage Association. So they decided to form a rival organization, which they called the National Woman's Suffrage Association. Mrs. Stanton served as the president of the new group for over 20 years.

The two rival women's rights groups were finally reunited in 1890 when the National American Woman's Suffrage Association was formed. Again Mrs. Stanton served as president, and again she stirred up trouble in the ranks. In order to strike back at men who based their arguments for the inequality of women upon the Bible, Elizabeth Stanton organized a committee to write *The Woman's Bible*. With the help of her committee, Mrs. Stanton wrote critical comments on each passage in the Bible that referred to the status of women. In the preface to the book, she urged that women be allowed to become ministers. The book was so outspoken that Mrs. Stanton's own organization voted not to be connected with it. Not to be stopped, Elizabeth Stanton continued her work and published a second volume in 1898.

Until the age of 77, Mrs. Stanton remained active in the women's rights movement. She then retired in New York City, but continued to write. A stout old woman with white curls, she died in 1902. She had achieved all that any man could have wished for—an education, a career, a family, and fame. And success eventually came for her also, for in 1920 women finally won the right to vote.

Susan B. Anthony

Susan B. Anthony

(1820-1906)

"No longer in the bloom of youth—if she ever had any bloom—hard-featured, cold as an icicle. . . ." This was a reporter's description of Susan Brownell Anthony, a reformer who worked for temperance, for the abolition of slavery, and, most important, for women's rights. Miss Anthony was no beauty, but she was one of the most influential women who ever stepped upon a speaker's platform.

Historians have often pictured Susan B. Anthony as a cold and stern product of her strict Quaker background. But she was also a woman of great intelligence and wit, a woman with a rebellious spirit. Susan inherited her rebellious spirit from her father, a Quaker who had dared to marry a Baptist woman. Unlike most men of his time, he believed that women had as much right to be educated and to earn a living as men. Susan's education, therefore, was a good one. A bright child, she had already learned to read and write at the age of three.

Susan did not plan to become a reformer, but she began to behave like one at an early age. At 17 she began a stormy career in teaching. For three years she was in charge of the instruction of girls at Canajoharie Academy in New York. Angered by sex discrimination in the teaching profession, she began battling for equal pay for women teachers, for coeducation, and for college training for girls. She was bold and outspoken, but her abilities were beyond doubt. "This woman," said one of the school's trustees, "is the smartest man that ever came to Canajoharie."

During her time at Canajoharie, Susan Anthony began attending lectures on various social reforms. She admired the reformers because they had the courage to speak out for the causes they believed in. Because she was opposed to liquor, Miss Anthony decided to join the temperance crusade. She possessed the courage and ability to become a leader in the movement. But she soon became painfully aware of her one great handicap: she was a woman. When Miss Anthony attempted to join the Sons of Temperance, a powerful temperance group, she was denied membership because of her sex. It was still considered improper for a woman to express her views before a public audience.

But Susan was not to be stopped. Since the Sons of Temperance would not have her, she organized the Daughters of Temperance—the first women's temperance organization in the United States. She went one step further in 1852 when she organized the Women's State Temperance Society in New York. As the powerful leader of two temperance groups, Susan Anthony was free to speak her mind.

Friends for over 40 years, Susan Anthony and Elizabeth Stanton founded the National Woman's Suffrage Association in 1869.

Like many other reformers, Miss Anthony did not confine her work to a single cause. The question of slavery was on everyone's mind, and in the 1850s Susan Anthony began crusading for abolition. But it was her introduction to Elizabeth Cady Stanton in 1851 that helped Susan decide upon her major area of reform—women's rights. Susan had often felt the sting of woman's position as a second-class citizen, and she was happy to join forces with Mrs. Stanton.

This was the beginning of her 40-year involvement in the women's rights movement.

The long, enduring friendship of Susan Anthony and Elizabeth Stanton was an important one to the feminist movement. Together they drove each other on despite many troubles. Susan was clear-thinking and logical, and she laid the groundwork for many of Elizabeth Stanton's speeches. She also saw to it that Elizabeth's interest in women's rights was not overcome by family affairs.

Unlike Lucy Stone, president of the American Woman's Suffrage Association, Susan Anthony and Elizabeth Stanton were radical in their views and methods. When the Fifteenth Amendment to the Constitution was passed, they opposed it because it gave the vote to freedmen without also giving it to women. Miss Anthony and Mrs. Stanton broke away from Lucy Stone's organization and established a more militant group of their own. In 1869 the National Woman's Suffrage Association was formed, with Elizabeth as the president and Susan as the vice-president.

Susan Anthony suffered one of the worst disappointments of her life in 1870, when her women's rights paper, *The Revolution*, fell into financial ruin. Susan began the paper in 1868 with the financial backing of George F. Train, a wealthy man impressed with Susan's devotion to the cause. The paper ended in 1870 when Mr. Train's money ran out. Miss Anthony was left not only with a bitter disappointment, but with a $10,000 debt as well.

Susan made the best of her failure. In order to pay off the debt, she lectured in city after city through extreme heat and cold. She eventually paid the debt in full. In doing this, she earned respect for both herself and the women's rights movement. One paper reported:

> She has done far better than the average businessman in like circumstances who would have settled for twenty cents on the dollar. Not Miss Anthony who pays her debts in full. She is fast growing to be the best argument for her cause of Woman Suffrage.

Front page from *The Revolution*, a short-lived women's rights paper established by Susan Anthony in 1868

Susan B. Anthony created national headlines in 1872 when she led a group of women to the polls in Rochester, New York, and was arrested for voting. Her trial and sentence to a fine (which she refused to pay) drew nationwide attention. Soon women across the nation were following in her footsteps. The Supreme Court finally stepped in and the case was decided against the women.

In the late 1880s Susan Anthony managed to bring the two rival women's rights organizations together again, after a 20-year separation. Under the guidance of Alice Blackwell, Lucy Stone's daughter, Susan met with Lucy in 1887.

Continuing Susan Anthony's crusade for women's rights, women campaign for the right to vote in Newark, New Jersey, 1914.

Together they worked to set aside the differences between their groups. Finally, in 1890, the National American Woman's Suffrage Association was formed, uniting the women at last. Susan served as vice-president until she replaced Mrs. Stanton as president two years later. She served as the organization's president from 1892 to 1900.

Miss Anthony died in 1906. She had lived to see women in Idaho, Colorado, Utah, and Wyoming achieve the right to vote; she had lived to see coeducation come to colleges; and she had lived to see her cause gain dignity and respect throughout the civilized world. Susan B. Anthony died a woman with great influence, loved and respected by thousands.

Amelia Jenks Bloomer

(1818-1894)

On September 18, 1851, the *New York Times* announced the arrival of the "bloomer costume" in that city. Five women had been seen on the streets wearing knee-length skirts over ankle-length pantaloons. Proper ladies were shocked to think that some women would set aside their flowing skirts and petticoats. Men were enraged. Was there no end to the female rebellion?

Amelia Bloomer never intended to start so much excitement with her new outfit. She first got the idea for the costume from a woman named Mrs. Charles Miller, who had designed a similar outfit for horseback riding. Amelia was so impressed with the outfit that she decided to make one for herself. When she wore it in downtown Seneca Falls, New York, the uproar began. Bloomers soon became one of the major issues of women's rights.

Although she became involved in the women's rights movement, Amelia Jenks Bloomer was basically a temperance reformer. She was convinced that alcohol was the curse of the nation. Her husband, Dexter C. Bloomer, was a young law student when Amelia met and married him. He wrote about Amelia's devotion to her principles when the couple was offered a wedding toast:

> Glasses were filled with the sparkling beverage and one of them was presented to her by the bridegroom himself, but she firmly yet pleasantly declined to accept it.
>
> 'What!' he said with the greatest earnestness. 'Will you not drink a glass with me on this joyful occasion? Surely it can do you no harm!'
>
> 'I cannot! I must not!'
>
> A crowd of guests standing around could but admire her great self-denial and devotion to principles. . . .

Once married, Amelia and her husband settled down in Seneca Falls, New York. In 1849 Amelia Bloomer became Seneca Fall's first woman deputy postmaster. She said she wanted to give a "practical demonstration of women's right to fill any place for which she had capacity." That same year she established *The Lily*, a powerful temperance magazine. In it, Amelia pointed out the evils related to drinking — suicides, accidents, murders, broken homes. The magazine

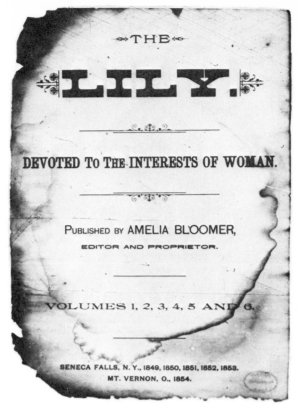

The Lily, a magazine which dealt with temperance and women's rights, was founded by Amelia Bloomer in 1849.

was a success, and it drew much attention and support to the temperance cause.

Due to the influence of Elizabeth Cady Stanton, Amelia decided to make some changes in *The Lily*. Up to this time, the magazine had dealt only with the temperance cause. But now, Amelia expanded it to include the cause of women's rights as well. *The Lily* thus became the first feminist magazine.

Amelia Bloomer, wearing the costume that
shocked the country

Then in 1851 Amelia Bloomer met Mrs. Charles Miller, the original creator of what later became known as the bloomer costume. What happened next is history. Recalling the experience. Amelia wrote ". . . . I had no idea of fully adopting the style; . . . no thought that my action would create an excitement throughout the civilized world. . . . This was all the work of the press."

A fashionable version of the bloomer costume

Although Mrs. Bloomer had not planned on creating such an uproar, she found herself enjoying the excitement caused by her new outfit. She began to lecture and crusade for dress reform, wearing her bloomers wherever she appeared. Soon famous women such as Mrs. Stanton and Lucy Stone jumped on the bandwagon and joined Amelia in wearing bloomers.

But most women continued to wear their long skirts and petticoats. Bloomers were not accepted despite the efforts of Amelia Bloomer, Lucy Stone, and Elizabeth Stanton—three of the most influential leaders of the women's rights movement. Mrs. Stanton wrote: "Had I counted the cost of the pantaloon costume, I would never have put it on. On, however, I'll never take it off, for now it involves a principle." But take it off she did. And so did the others. Bloomers were simply not worth the endless laughing and yelling from the crowds. Besides, the women agreed that the costume was drawing attention away from the truly important goal—achieving equality for women.

In 1853 Amelia Bloomer sold *The Lily* and went westward with her husband, settling in Ohio and later in Iowa. Without her successful magazine, Amelia's life changed. The Bloomers adopted two children, and Amelia became a devoted mother and housewife. She wore her bloomer costume only for housework. Until her death in 1894, she lived a full, rich life.

Amelia Jenks Bloomer contributed much to the causes of temperance and women's rights during her lifetime, but she was to be remembered best for her contribution to the world of fashion. Mrs. Miller had first created the bloomer, but Amelia's name was to be forever associated with it.

General Neal Dow

Neal Dow

(1804-1897)

Neal Dow was born in Portland, Maine, in 1804. His parents were Quakers, and he was raised very strictly. Neal's mother helped him see his mission in life most clearly: "By her I was taught to abhor the very idea of liquor drinking, and at her feet...I came to believe that to be indifferent to the welfare of others was a sin and a shame."

Where liquor was concerned, Neal Dow became a fanatic. He did not merely call for moderation in the use of liquor; he wanted the sale and use of liquor completely banned. Dow saw liquor as the curse that tied the poor to their hardship and misery. He decided that by helping to prohibit the sale and use of liquor, he would be helping the poor. He had learned his mother's lesson well.

Neal Dow's war against liquor began actively at the age of 24, when he made his first speech for prohibition. When the Maine State Temperance Society held its first convention, Neal Dow was there as a delegate. But as the years passed, he became more and more dissatisfied with the society. He felt it was weak and ineffective. Unlike others in the society, Dow wanted complete prohibition. So in 1838 he established a stricter organization, the Maine Temperance Union. Dow believed merely preaching that drinking was immoral would get the temperance cause nowhere. Political action was needed.

And political action was what Neal Dow got. In 1851 he prepared the famous "Maine Law," a much stronger liquor law than the one passed in 1846. The passage of Dow's law brought complete prohibition to Maine. Neal Dow had lectured and worked hard for the law, and its passage made him a hero—at least to the non-drinking public.

A general in the Union army, Dow was wounded and imprisoned during the Civil War.

Political victories were not over for Dow. Soon after his prohibition law was passed, he was elected mayor of Portland, a position which he held from 1851 to 1859. As Portland's newly elected mayor, Dow decided to drive all the bootleggers (people who illegally made and sold liquor) out of the city. He personally led raid after raid, cracking bottles and kegs with an axe. In one night alone, he and his followers poured over $2,000 worth of whiskey into the gutters in front of the city hall.

The Civil War temporarily turned Dow's attention away from prohibition. As a Quaker, Dow was not supposed to take part in war or violence. But his hatred of slavery led him to enlist in the Union army. Dow, who rose to the rank of general, was wounded, captured, and imprisoned during the war. When he returned home, he was hailed as a hero.

In 1880 Neal Dow ran unsuccessfully as the Prohibition party's candidate for president of the United States. He died 17 years later, in 1897. Intelligent and energetic, Dow was a reformer of great ability. Unfortunately, he devoted most of his life to a cause that eventually failed. And Neal Dow, too, failed—failed to realize that liquor was only one of the many problems of the poor.

Julia Ward Howe
(1819-1910)

Mine eyes have seen the glory of the coming
  of the Lord;
He is trampling out the vintage where the grapes
  of wrath are stored;
He hath loosed the fateful lightning of His
  terrible, swift sword;
His truth is marching on.
Glory! Glory! Hallelujah! Glory! Glory! Hallelujah!
Glory! Glory! Hallelujah! His truth is marching on!

Julia Ward Howe wrote these famous words early one morning in November 1861, shortly after the beginning of the Civil War. The day before, she had visited some Union army camps outside of Washington, D.C., and had watched as Union troops marched into battle. The moving scene of men going into battle inspired Julia to write "The Battle Hymn of the Republic."

Julia Ward Howe

She later described how she awoke before dawn and began writing the hymn to the melody of the popular song "John Brown's Body."

I searched for a sheet of paper and an old stump of a pen which I had had the night before and began to scrawl the lines almost without looking, as I had learned to do by often scratching down verses in the darkened room where my little children were sleeping. Having completed this, I lay down again and fell asleep, but not without feeling that something of importance had happened to me.

The sight of Union troops marching into battle inspired Julia Ward Howe to write "The Battle Hymn of the Republic," one of the most famous songs of the Civil War.

"The Battle Hymn of the Republic" changed Julia Howe's life. It was published in the *Atlantic Monthly* in the spring of 1862. The hymn quickly caught the attention of the North and soon became the most popular song of the Union forces. As her majestic hymn rose to fame, so did Julia.

However, Mrs. Howe was not unknown even before she wrote her famous work. She was born in 1819 to one of New York City's most famous and wealthy families. At the age of 24 she married Dr. Samuel Gridley Howe, an outspoken reformer and a man considerably older than she. Julia's family disapproved. But Julia wanted to share Howe's exciting life. She moved with him to Boston soon after they were married. In Boston she associated with her husband's circle of friends and developed her literary talents by writing poems and plays.

Julia Howe became involved in several reform movements during her lifetime. Like her husband, she spent much of her time crusading for the abolition of slavery. Both Julia and her husband worked as editors of the Boston *Commonwealth*, an abolitionist paper. When the Civil War ended and the slaves were finally freed, Julia Howe began to look for another cause to support.

Earlier in her life, Mrs. Howe had found the women's rights movement undignified. But Lucy Stone—the first president of the American Woman's Suffrage Association—persuaded her to join the cause in the 1860s. Mrs. Howe became a strong supporter of the women's rights movement and eventually served as the first president of the New England Woman's Suffrage Association. Because Mrs. Howe was associated with it, the feminist movement gained a certain degree of respect. An observer wrote to one of Mrs. Howe's daughters: "Your mother's great importance to this cause is that she forms a bridge between the world of society and the world of reform."

In addition to writing her famous hymn, Julia Ward Howe was involved in many reform movements during her lifetime, including women's rights and the abolition of slavery.

In addition to women's rights, Julia was interested in the cause of world peace. She organized the American section of the Woman's International Peace Association. Mrs. Howe's devotion to this cause also led her to establish the first Mother's Day, in 1872, as a day dedicated to world peace. For several years after, annual Mother's Day meetings were held in Boston under the leadership of Julia Howe.

When she died in 1910, Julia Ward Howe was one of the most famous women in America. She had been the first woman ever elected to the American Academy of Arts and Letters; she had supported a number of important social causes; she had written "The Battle Hymn of the Republic"; and she had been a great lady.

Anthony Comstock

Anthony Comstock
(1844-1915)

The reformer Anthony Comstock was a man who spent his whole life fighting evil and vice. His main targets of attack were drinking, gambling, and pornography—literature and art intended to arouse sexual desire. To some people, Comstock was a great moral crusader. To writers, artists, and publishers, however, he was a narrow-minded busybody.

Comstock was born in Connecticut in 1844. After high school he took a job as a store clerk. One day a dog went mad outside the store and young Comstock was forced to shoot it. The dog's owner was a drunk who had just traded stolen groceries for whiskey. In Comstock's opinion, the whiskey was the cause of the entire situation. He burst into the liquor store, smashing bottles and pouring the liquor on the floor.

Throughout his life, Anthony Comstock remained violently opposed to everything he considered immoral. After serving in the Union army and then working in business, he took up moral crusading as a full-time occupation. Moral crusading was often dangerous. For example, Comstock once had two publishers arrested for printing what he considered to be pornography. Six years later, one of the publishers struck back. He slashed Comstock's face with a knife, scarring him for life. To cover up the terrible scar, Comstock grew a beard.

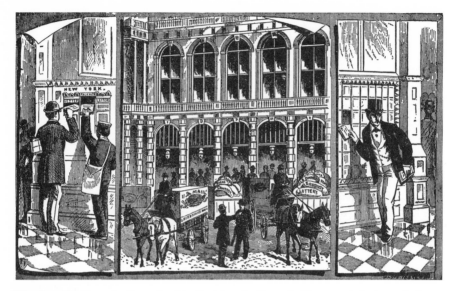

The frontispiece to Comstock's first book, *Frauds Exposed*. *Left*, evil-doers mail obscene literature. *Center*, the New York Post Office with mail bags containing the literature. *Right*, a gentleman picks up his obscene mail.

In 1868 Comstock wrote a detailed New York law forbidding the publishing and selling of immoral works. The passage of this law was a major victory for Comstock and his crusade against vice. But he achieved his most lasting reforms five years later. In 1873 he fought for and won stricter federal postal laws to ban immoral literature from the mails. In the same year he organized the New York Society for the Suppression of Vice. The formation of the Watch and Ward Society of Boston was also inspired by Comstock. Both societies were dedicated to stamping out pornography.

The seal shown above was adopted by the Society for the Suppression of Vice and used on its stationery. On the left, a man convicted of selling pornography is jailed. On the right, a gentleman destroys immoral literature.

In his later years, Comstock carried out many raids against publishers, booksellers, gamblers, artists—anyone he felt was involved with vice. Shortly before his death in 1915, he proudly announced that during his career he had destroyed about 160 tons of literature and pictures.

Anthony Comstock inspired the playwright George Bernard Shaw to originate the word "comstockery." This word refers to the destruction of literature and art considered dangerous to public morals. Comstock destroyed tons of literature during his lifetime, but because of him the English language became one word richer.

Jane Addams

Jane Addams

(1860-1935)

One of the most dedicated and accomplished social reformers of the 19th century was Jane Addams. At a time when most women reformers were working for the right to vote or for the temperance cause, Jane had one aim—to lessen the suffering of the poor.

Jane was born in 1860 to Quaker parents in Cedarville, Ohio. Her father was a banker and a man of understanding and wisdom. Jane's home life was comfortable and happy, except for one problem: Jane was sick much of the time.

After suffering from typhoid fever, she became ill with an even more serious disease—tuberculosis of the spine. In spite of her illness, Jane attended Rockford College in Illinois. There she was an editor of the college magazine and president of her class. When she graduated in 1882, Jane Addams was the top student in her class.

After college Jane went to Philadelphia to study medicine. But she pushed herself too hard. Again troubled with her spine, she was confined to bed for months. After this long period of illness and inactivity, she decided to take a trip to Europe. She traveled with a college friend, Ellen Starr. This trip was to be one of the most important influences in Jane's life.

A visit to a poor section of London made a lasting impression on Jane. There she watched as a heap of rotten vegetables was auctioned off to a crowd of poor people. She saw one hungry old man eat a rotten cabbage, and she was sickened. This experience, along with a visit to a London settlement house (a center which offered help and education to the poor), gave Jane an idea. Perhaps she could find meaning in her life by helping the poor, desperate people in her own country.

In 1889 Jane Addams established Hull House, a settlement house which became widely known for its work with the poor.
(Courtesy Chicago Historical Society)

After returning to the United States, Jane Addams and her friend Ellen Starr set about the task of establishing a settlement house for the poor, immigrant population of Chicago. Charles J. Hull, one of the wealthiest men in Chicago, donated his spacious old mansion for the cause. The doors of Hull House were first opened to the public in 1889. Jane Addams served as the head resident of the settlement house until her death in 1935.

Once established, Hull House became many things to many people. Sometimes called the first "neighborhood center" in America, it served as a place for Chicago's poor to meet and to find help for their problems. Children had a

Jane Addams talking to a child at Hull House

place to play. Families without a place to bathe could come every week to bathe at Hull House. Games, debates, handicrafts, and civic affairs brought the people of the overcrowded Chicago neighborhood together at Hull House. These people soon discovered that they liked their neighbors, and, more important, that they liked themselves.

Jane Addams was not satisfied to sit back and watch the activities at Hull House. Instead, she and Ellen Starr trained and encouraged new leaders to take their place and carry on their work. In addition, Miss Addams spoke to influential groups of people about the importance of social work and trained social workers. She persuaded these people that social reforms were needed and organized them into powerful civic groups.

Jane Addams lectured throughout the United States on many social problems, including child labor, public health, and unemployment relief. The need for research into the causes of poverty and crime was another frequent topic of her lectures. She fought for such social reforms as the first law limiting working hours for women and the first state child-labor law. Housing reform was yet another of her causes.

Miss Addams lived to the age of 75. In her last years she devoted herself to the cause of world peace. She served as the president of the Women's International League of Peace and Freedom from 1915 to 1929. For all her efforts, she was awarded the Nobel Peace Prize in 1931. Four years later, she died.

By the time Jane Addams died, she had accomplished what she had set out to do—she had found meaning in her life by helping the poor. She had spent her life in the service of others—the mark of a true reformer.